# Gardens of Havana, Cuba

A TRAVEL PHOTO ART BOOK

LAINE CUNNINGHAM

Gardens of Havana, Cuba

A Travel Photo Art Book

Published by Sun Dogs Creations
*Changing the World One Book at a Time*
Print ISBN: 978-1-951389-14-7

Cover Image by Laine Cunningham
Cover Design by Angel Leya

Copyright © 2024 Laine Cunningham

All rights reserved. No part of this book may be reproduced in any form or by any means, electronic, mechanical, digital, photocopying or recording, except for the inclusion in a review, without permission in writing from the publisher.

Havana, Cuba's tropical climate makes it perfect for people who love gardening. Many homes in neighborhoods like Vedado and Miramar are fronted with flowers and shrubs that provide year-round visual interest. Common showy picks include arrowhead plants, seagrape, and the multicolored garden croton.

Deeper into the layers, red frangipani and hibiscus send color streaming above flame-of-the-woods shrubs. Fire plants and ground ivy dot smaller gardens, while volunteer chase trees wave like streamers. Guava trees and banana palms add to a garden's utility.

Blooming beauties include the shaving brush tree, bloodflower, peacock flower, cat's tail, and the bush clock vine. The jasmine called the mariposa flower, or the butterfly flower, is a popular choice as the national flower.

Now take a private tour in *Gardens of Havana, Cuba*.

ALCAZAR

SOL

FENG SHUI

GUARDIAN

SOLITUDE

CARDINAL

CORRIDOR

BELOVED

SITTING ROOM

SAINT

MORNING AFTER

OVERLAP

BOO

LAPPETS

CATHEAD

WICKET

SKYGATE

FULLSCREEN

CINDER

JANUS

JIGSAW

SHOAL

LEE

CLASSIC

AIRSTRIP

GODZILLA

EVENTUALLY

PRINCESS

RANK AND FILE

GENTLE

PISTACHIO

PINNACLES

CALIPSO

WISE

TANGO

SCRABBLE

RAVE

PENUMBRA

WINGED

SHUSH

RUMBA

DAZZLE

PERSIMMON

## TITLES IN THIS SERIES

Havana, Cuba
Old Havana, Cuba
The Malecon, Havana, Cuba
Central Havana, Cuba
Vedado, Havana, Cuba
Regla, Havana, Cuba
Miramar, Havana, Cuba
Streets of Havana, Cuba
Classic Cars of Cuba
Classic Cars of Old Havana, Cuba
Classic Cars of Havana, Cuba
Spanish Colonial Havana, Cuba
Gardens of Havana, Cuba
Verge Gardens of Havana, Cuba
Cats of Havana, Cuba
Colón Cemetery, Cuba
Havana Art School

www.ingramcontent.com/pod-product-compliance
Lightning Source LLC
Chambersburg PA
CBHW040002080526
44586CB00027B/2850